Tales of Perception
Vol. I

LaDell L. Brown

Table of Contents

"One day you will tell your story of how you've overcame what you're going through now, and it will become someone else's survival guide."

- Brene Brown

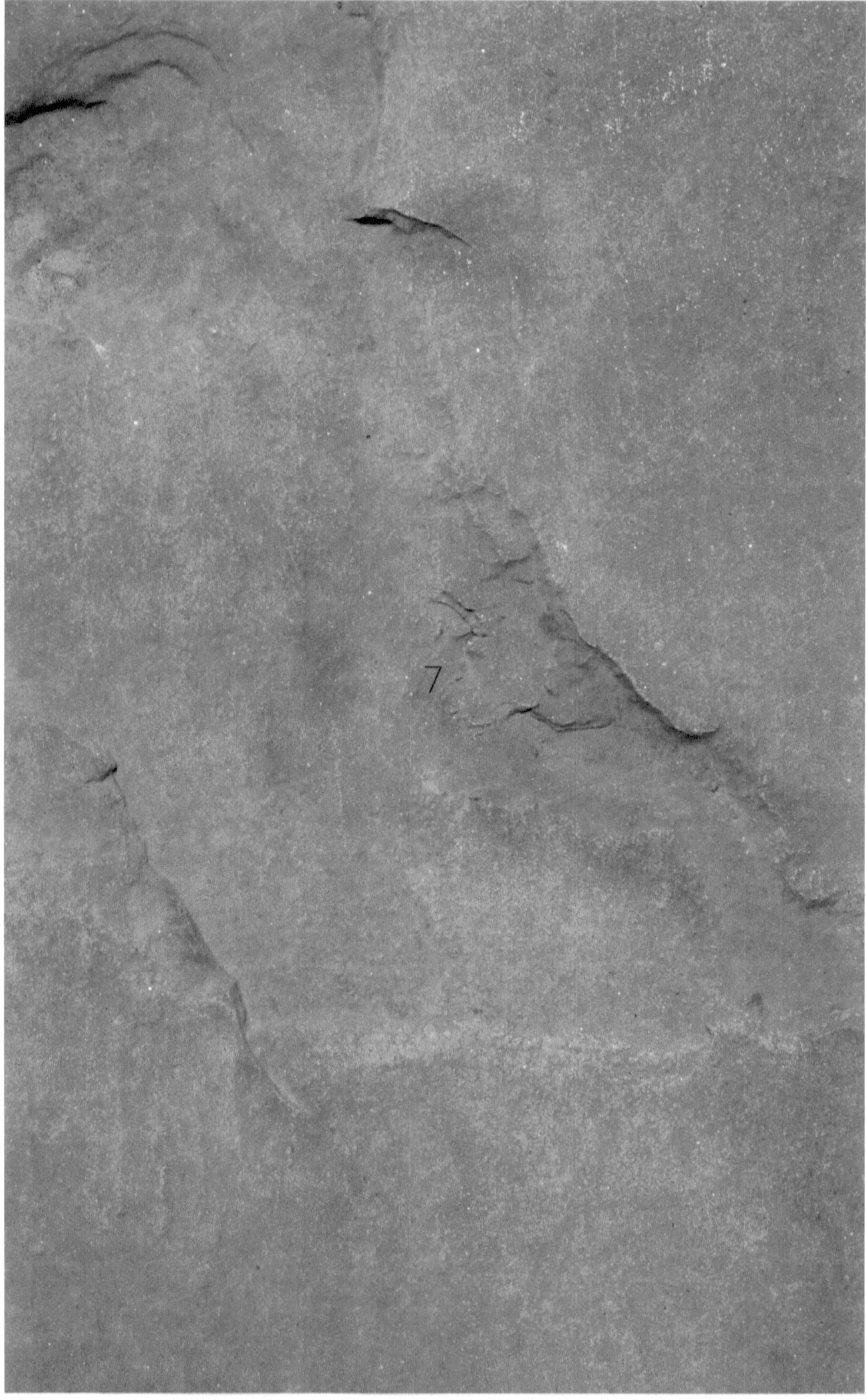

Good Guy
vs
Bad Guy

We walk the same path
but got on different shoes.
Why do bad guys win
and good guys lose.

You tell me all your wants.
I'm who you come to so you can confide.
When will it be time to take action?
Why is the good guy constantly thrown aside?

The best way to hide something
is to keep it in plain sight.
So since I'm always available,
is that why you can't see the light?

Why can't we make this last forever?
Why do you only want the good guy when you
finally decide there is nothing better?

I'm not a last resort.
I'm certainly not gonna wait.
When you finally realize you want to share my path,
it will be too late.

We walk the same path
but got on different shoes.
Why do bad guys win
and good guys lose?

Alone

As I get lost looking into the sky
asking myself why,
why have I allowed myself to be comforted
by what are really just good lies?

Not judged by what happens to me
more so by how I react,
I chose to take accountability
and took my life back.

At times I have become motivated
for the sake of proving people wrong,
while the answers for success
were inside of me all along.

Ignore the criticism
from those who mean no good.
During my ascension
it was alone I stood.

Whats Next?

While the grass shines green
and the wind courageously blows,
on the life path destined for me,
my travel is still ways to go.

Driven by the encouragement
from the voice deep within,
as my consciousness grows,
I start to lose friends.

From the people I love,
to the people I hate.
From the people I see in disgust,
to the colleagues whose hands I shake.

Time and time again
the world I inhabit tends to show,
that nothing last forever.
Everything comes and goes.

Don't hold on to the past,
a bright future awaits.
In order to get your next meal
you must first clean your plate.

Questions

Entrapped by my own thoughts
I become stuck in a rut.
Weighed down by the burden of pain
with no desire to even get up.

Is this the life destined?
Is there no more hope?
Do I project my pain onto others?
Would anyone care if I spoke?

My emotions run high.
The pain burns deep.
Nowhere to run.
The pain must be set free.

Greatness

Do you understand what it takes to be great?
All the friends you lose,
All the enemies you make.

Nothing seems to work out as planned
but that doesn't stop your drive.
The ultimate goal,
release the greatness you suppress inside.

Don't feel bad for being different,
you are only different to those who don't
understand.
Many roadblocks will stand before you,
steadily tempting you to give in.

Be great and blaze your own path,
those behind will soon follow.
Don't ever compromise to fit in.

Living someone else's dream for you is
certainly not the way.
Start to unlock your greatness,
today.

Picture Perfect

Time to take a stand
against those who cause me pain.
None of it makes sense,
yet no one is really the blame.

Things aren't always
what they seem to be.
While blinded by success,
the tunnel vision keeps me at peace.

So many obstacles.
No room for error.
Soon all eyes shall open,
To a picture much clearer.

The Little Things

Small yet significant,
undervalued in the role it plays,
something not given much attention to,
yet affects you drastically if gone missing
today.

Difficult to gauge
something you didn't know you need.
It serves its purpose daily,
though you really have to look for it in order
to see.

It diminishes in value
since it doesn't sparkle and it's not the most
flash.
Looking at things long term though,
it's the only thing that's built to last.

Don't look past it
because other things appear to stand out.
Make sure to celebrate the little things,
since these are the things we can't live
without.

Be Yourself

Lost.....in a world driven by sin.
My identity isn't what I imagined it to be.
The ways things are going on in my life,
I just scream to the heavens to set me free.

Why is this happening to me?
I know I can't be only one.
But it feels like I'm so alone,
the life destined for me has yet begun.

Lost.
Is the only word where I can identify but what
does it really mean?
Is it my own fault or is it my surroundings
that makes it really hard to be me?

Peer pressure feels impossible to escape
from.
All I want to feel is accepted.
So I do things I know is wrong
and just live later to regret it.

I have own voice
but I'm afraid to share it

because of the resentment of others
and sometimes my parents.

I'm so lost in this world of mines.
I hide away in my own thoughts.
I'm the only one who understands me
but at what cost?

As time goes by I grow to understand,
my life experiences and perception
is the driving force of who I really am.

Wanting to be like famous celebrities
was all I inspired to be.
But as long as I give anything I do my all
and be the leader pf my own life,
I guarantee you people will grow up
wanting to be like
ME!

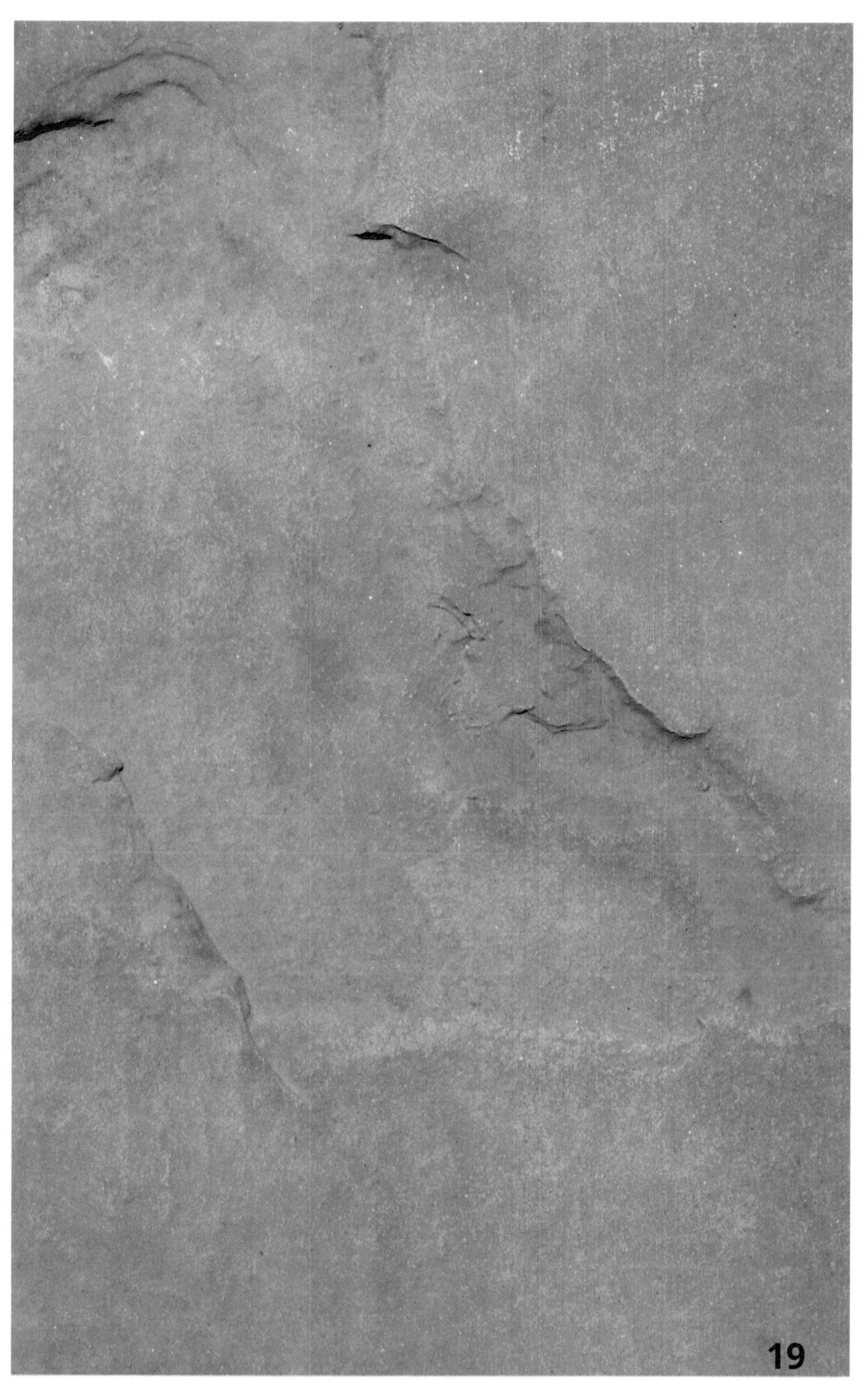

Why Me?

Constantly engulfed into others pain.
Always there when anyone needs help.
When it's time to finally look my way,
those same people tend to be just for self.

Without anyone to turn to,
without anyone willing to listen,
without anyone willing to hold me up
when there is obviously something missing.

Over and over I hear
"It's gonna be ok" and " Stay Strong".
The whole time
I just needed to know I was welcome in your home.

I don't ask for much,
which is maybe why help is still hidden.
I expect things from people
who don't even know expectations have been given.

Thr Night Off

Tonight is your night off.
Tonight I'm in control.
Let the seduction take over.
Feel the rush through your toes.

Slowly I caress, never missing a spot.
Unlocking all the stress,
giving it everything I got.

Aggressive yet gentle,
I've landed in your mental,
helping you get through,
the hard week you just been to.

Welcome to your night off,
where the intense feeling shall overcome.
You may have the night off
but things will still be done.

So let me be the one
to make you come back,
to your next night off.